'OUR MAGICAL D

by

ANNETTE McFARLINE

FOREWORD

ANNETTE McFARLINE lives today on the Hampshire/Dorset border and divides her time between her beloved New Forest and the Dorset countryside and coast. A keen walker and pony trekker, photographer and writer the production of 'OUR MAGICAL DORSET' has enabled her to enjoy all of these pastimes to the full.

She is a person of many parts. Widely experienced in the Fashion and Beauty world, she also holds a Diploma in Crisis Counselling and has proved to be an interesting and entertaining after dinner speaker.

An acclaimed writer of poetry, short stories and feature articles, Annette finds real inspiration from our land. She believes we lead the world in literature and poetry because we lead the world in beauty and, nowhere is this more prolific than in this corner of the world from which she writes. Annette's words are enhanced by her full-colour photographs celebrating the beauty of Dorset which must surely be one of England's loveliest counties.

'OUR MAGICAL DORSET' is the sequel to the very popular 'MY NEW FOREST' which has found its way into every corner of the world.

WELCOME TO DORSETSHIRE

Across the New Forest border
Sweet Dorset bids her welcome
Mudeford Quay and Christchurch' homely Priory
To the exhilerating air and space of Hengistbury Head
The rugged coastline falling rough and tumble
To the smooth Bournemouth Chines
And so on to the bustling harbour of Poole
A landmark that stands in the track of past time ....
Turning inland from the Coast seek ye Wimborne, Cranborne, and beyond
The quiet undulating countryside so rich in history
Where rivers wind and work their magic through lush green meadows
While names touch and play harmonies with the heartstrings
Canford Magna, Corfe Mullen, Furzehill and Badbury Rings ....

THIS OLD DORSET CHURCHYARD

This old Dorset churchyard with gravestones askew
Where overgrown grasses jostle the mighty yews
Here rest the people who in days gone by
Created this village for today, you and I ....
The monument in the corner dedicated to the Squire
Stands testimony to a time when fair play was required
His word was the law and bore no other
While folk lived in harmony one with another ....
Today as we stand on this sacred soil
We stand among men unafraid of their toil
Men of the village who could reap, sow or thatch
Skilled men of the land, today hard to match ....
Things must have been different in those far off days
Imagine just horses and carts .... slow gentle ways
Working long and hard the days for their crust
Six days of the week from dawn until dusk ....
Their women must have been hardy and capable
Good housekeepers, cooks, so willing and able
To look after their menfolk as they in turn taught
Not much time in their day for one selfish thought ....
Sunday would be cherished as such a Special Day
A day for rest and peace and play
Church and Sunday School would be a must
For the villagers here who have now turned to dust ....

POOLE

The colour, the noise, the bustle of Poole
Excites the spirit with its ever new
Where old and modern jostle together
The past and the present combines pure endeavour ....
From the high street shops of today
Search ye the back streets and beyond
Where narrow lanes and houses
Boast whispers of days long gone
Here history bids a welcome
A testament that will ever last
Where sweeping skirts and buckled shoes
Strolled the cobbles of the past ....
Poole Quay breathes its secrets
Of the days of long ago
While today the holidaymakers linger
Where the ferries steam and flow
Fishing boats and heaving nets again recall the time
When pirates and smugglers wrought their deeds
In the days before yours and mine
The scent of tar, seaweed and salt
Are the same as they were back then
While we wonder 'are we so very changed'
From those tough seafaring men
Poole Quay's character is undiminished
With an enchantment that never tires
And amid the network of winding streets
The bells of St. James' inspire.

THE SEA

Breathe the air and taste the salt
And feel the spirits rise
Why is it when upon the sea we gaze
We are always caught by surprise
Do we forget how blue it is
How breathtaking to our eyes
The wide expanse that is ever free
Reflecting the mighty skies.

There is no greater balm to a weary soul
Than the symphony of waves lapping to shore
The melodic consistency in a changing world
Lays foundation to Nature's score
Nothing can rival the majesty of rocks
That are lashed with a snowy surf
The exquisite harmony of sun and sea
Glimpses for all a heaven on earth.

LONELINESS

There are times in every one's life
When all alone we feel
Not just a passing solo day
But the hours when dark loneliness is real
At times like this there's no escape
We don't want to be at home
Or find ourselves within a crowd
The feelings loom overgrown
Friendships of the past remind us
Of how empty life is today
For somehow it is with those we've lost
Who appear as the sun's golden rays.

And what of the future before us
When will this loneliness pass
Will we again enjoy companionship
Or must this loneliness last ....
There is no time limit on sadness
No contract drawn on tears
No man is an island so they say
And sometimes it must take years
To feel free of the heavy burden
Of facing life all alone
While watching others hand in hand
Recalls happy times we've known.

It's so easy, we think, for others
Who have families to which they turn
But families can be so difficult
As many of us have learned ....
Yet some times when there's just no-one
When life is too much to bear
We remember our Heavenly Father
And suddenly life's not so unfair
For He is always with us
Forever by our side
The best friend we could ever have
In Heavenly Love abide.

WITH THANKS

There are scenes which once witnessed are never forgotten
That bring a tear to the eye and a tingle to the skin
Scenes which will revisit the subconscious at any unbidden moment
For their beauty is a heavenly thing ....
Who would stand on the green Purbeck Hills above Corfe and not
be filled with awe
Whose eyes could rest upon the Stour Valley and not give thanks
Who could watch the sea thunder on the mighty cliffs of Lulworth
Gaze upon the hard limestone twisted and worn by wave and fate
While Durdle Door arches its back into a perfect natural gate ....
Who can watch the blue grey and white of the swirling waters
Or watch the entwined sea and surf somersault on Dancing Ledge
Who can witness all of these without a hand laying claim upon
the heart ....
All who visit Dorset my friend.

WHERE THE PAST WHISPERS

Whispers from the essence of Old Dorset
Abound to the traveller alone
Where cobbled streets and houses
Boast bow windows and purbeck stone
They remind us of a past that is ancient
That is shrouded in grey mystery
While three-penny-piece roofs of thatch or stone
Stand steeped in a rich history.

Dorchester acclaims Thomas Hardy
As we walk in the footsteps of 'Tess'
Where highwayman once rode the highways
How they terrorised folk in the west
These long-forgotten centuries are but a thought away
The past suddenly becomes the present
While the future's anchored at bay.

The smugglers return in their galleons
To plunder this coastline so dear
While the dreams of the traveller can almost relive
The adventure, the treachery, the fear
Of those who were lured to their tragic ends
By the robbers and thieves of the waves
Whilst the years are washed away in their blood
As we visit the Past here today.

FOR IN A GARDEN

They say that in a garden you are nearest of all to God
Amongst the trees and shrubs that bloom from your hand
He is there by your side to listen
To soothe and completely understand ....
For in each of your border flowers
And in every newly mown lawn
The beauty of God is present
At twilight time or dawn
So sweep, my friend, your garden paths to brush all worries astray
Water your flowers with diligence to drown all your own cares away
Thank God for His love and His promise
Remembering that tomorrow is another day
In summer heat take the time to sit and rest
Feel the peace of God in the sunshine
Allow your mind to run free and clear
Whispering thanks for your own sweet garden
For remember, He is near ....
Feed the birds in the chill of winter
When your garden is a fairyland of snow
Rake autumn leaves with vigorous love
Cherish lovingly every newly formed bud ....
Assist Mother Nature with a helping hand
Taming unruly growth and determined weeds
Thus making your garden a Special Place
To sleep perchance to dream.

CHILDHOOD

Friends we may choose along the way
Family members we are largely stuck
Some of us are born more fortunate
It is largely a matter of luck ....

Were you like me a product of love
Who grew up in a happy home
Where flowers bloomed and life was safe ....
Father and Grandfather were handsome and tall
While Mother and Nan the fairest of all
Summer days were gloriously long and hot
Every day an adventure in meadows and copse ....
On winter nights Grandfather would tell us such tales
His eyes full of mischief with his old pipe in his hand
Stories of war years and strange foreign lands
While Nan would be smiling, knitting, shaking her head
"It's high time you, young lady, were ready for bed"
And Dad would be listening to his favourite tunes
Singing sweetly along 'How High The Moon'
Were you like me .... with a best friend for a Mum
A lady you admired, strict, but so much fun
We would bicycle, picnic and laugh all the way
So sunny, so safe, were those far off days ....

I hope your childhood was like that for you
So that when you look back the skies are bright blue
But if they were not then remember, my friend,
It's never too late to begin life again
Make the best of today – a memory to last
Look always to the future and not to the past
Make this day into a memory you'll never forget
Pleasurable moments enjoyed with no regrets
You're never too old to start life anew
So that when you look back your skies are blue too.

SPRINGTIME IN DORSET

Butterflies dancing in the sun
All God's creatures having fun
Caterpillars crawling by
While singing bluebirds fill our county's skies
Honeybees beset the Blandford flowers
While Lytchett Matravers is washed by gentle showers
Where emerald grass sparkles freshly mown
The velvet carpet of sweet Dorset's home
Daffodils of gold and bluebells fair
Springtime comes to Bere Regis bringing a soft and fragrant air
Lighter the Shapwick nights
Longer the Lulworth days
Where trees are pink with blossom
And hedgerows are white with May
Pause by a woodland's trickling stream
Gaze in awe at the rolling Chesil sea
Laugh with the playful tides of Springtime ....
Fish for supper on Weymouth Quay.

THE COLOUR OF SPRINGTIME

Forget-me-nots and late daffodils jostle with jonquil
While the white heather towers above them all
Bluebells and white bells tall, upright and slim
Rosey tulips open to show golden rings within.

Pale lemon sweetly smile the primrose
Purple and pink sprawl the majestic azaleas
Sweet buds that welcome the sunshine rays
On this pure heavenly April day.

Blossoms of pale and brightest ruby abound
And snowy opal buds open without a murmur
Soon the scarlet rhododendrons will burst with glorious might
While human hearts are gladdened and suddenly oh, so light.

Lengthening days are at last filled with sun
From dawn till dusk, till day is done
Birds welcome the Spring at break of day
Oh, lovely month, this month of May ....

SWANAGE

I'm observing the trippers to Swanage
It's such an education, you know,
Watching them walk and talk and play
On this sunny early Summer day
There's a variety of dress to start with
Some are stripped right to the core
While others play safe with thick sweaters
Anoraks, trousers and more ....
All walks of life and ages are together mingled here
And to a man they have one aim
To enjoy Bank Holiday once again ....
The sky is clear without a cloud
The sea is a brilliant blue
Voices and laughter ride the waves
As I sit quietly with attentive gaze
Observing this holiday view.

I wonder what has gone on in their lives before today
Has illness pitted their pathway
Or unhappiness marred the way
What worries do they harbour
But today have pushed aside
Are they fearful of the future
Or will they face it in their stride ....
Have they argued with their neighbour
Have they money problems with which to deal
Are they on holiday here in Swanage
Or do they live quite near ....
I wonder how many have lost a dear one
Who know what it is to grieve
How many have felt so desperate
This life they would willingly leave ....

And I sit and I watch and I ponder
As the masses wander along
That whatever troubles have dogged their way
They are here with a holiday song ....
As young and old relax in the sunshine
All worries are clean swept aside
No room for concern or care today
Farewell to Life's ebb tide
Tomorrow, of course, will be different
But tomorrow must take care of its own
Enjoy this day the Lord has made
To recall it with gladness at home.

THE FAITHFUL ONES

There are a faithful few who work behind the scenes of life
They show concern for others
Hoping to ease another's strife
To make life easier for their neighbour
Visit those who are in need
While often they are never thanked
For their thoughtful, kindly deed
There are a faithful few who work almost in disguise
Visiting the sick in hospital
Where time is slow to fly
They're always there to lend a hand
Offering help with such a willingness
While oftentimes their joyful ways
Masks their own unhappiness
There are a faithful few who work despite the trials of their own
Who find a sweet contentment
That is not always to be found at home
But they find an escape – pushing their cares far away
When others seek and need their help
They are the good samaritans of today
There are a faithful few whose work will never entirely end
Who will continue to work for the good of others
Helping happiness transcend
Working as directed by a kind and loving Lord
Casting proverbial rain clouds into sunshine
With the peace of God as their reward.

WH481
WH 239
LI 133

A DORSET SOLDIER

I'm sitting alone on the cliff top
My jacket I've tossed to one side
It's warm up here in the sunshine
Watching the outgoing tide
The sky is as blue as a cornflower
The rocks are whiter than snow
A day that's meant to treasure
But my thoughts are of long ago ....
The tide that is ebbing the distant
Is laying my life on the sand
My beloved Mother is with me again
And suddenly there's dear old Dad
What carefree days they were back then
When life was simple and new
Dad was my hero and Mum was 'my gal'
I was so proud - I hope they knew ....
At outbreak of war Dad went to fight
"For Dorset and England" he said
He returned to us a broken man
Some said he should have been dead
But Mum nursed him and gave him such loving care
That eventually he was more like the same
How helpless I'd felt in those long dark days
My Dad could only whisper my name ....
The day he felt better we had iced cakes for tea
It's silly the things you recall
And that night I watched the sun go down
'Ah, there is a God after all' ....
Eventually Dad and I could resume our walks
On the cliffs where we used to play
He said that nature is the best tonic of all
And you'd find him up here every day
I would come with him when ever I could
Best pals we would always be
"Dad and his lad" Mum would laughingly quip
I was so glad that lad was me!
He'd speak of his dad and grandfather too
"All good Dorset stock" he would say
"Be proud of your country, my son,
We fought for your freedom today" ....

Then he'd look sad and my heart would ache
He was remembering his friends lost in war
His face would grow grey and the eyes would grow dim
A sight I'll remember forever more ....
My Father and Mother are long since gone
And I live alone in our home
I walk these cliffs every day of my life
Up here I am never alone ....
I went to France and saw where he fought
Where those friends are who never returned
Dad fought bravely for Dorset and England
Though in battle he was so badly burned
I've reaped the benefit of Dad's war
And I'll treasure these white Dorset cliffs as he said
But I shall never forget the fields of France ....
And those millions of poppies of red.

The Old Granary
Restaurant
Restaurant
NO

YOURS SINCERELY

I am all alone in this garden
My head touching the back of my chair
With the sun so warm upon my face
I have not a solitary care
The garden is fragrant with sweetness
White lilac perfumes the air
While a breeze tiptoes through the treetops
Kissing softly the fringe of my hair ....
I close my eyes to listen
To singing birds and the buzzing of bees
And am filled with such pure gratitude
What have I done to deserve all of these ....
Suddenly through the warmth and perfume
A voice whispers low and clear
'Because you are a child of God's Family
And there is nothing that you need fear'.

SWEET DORSET

Sweet Dorset Shire of pure delight
From Durlston Head to Studland Bay
Picturesque waters on which to ferry
To Wareham, Bridport and Abbotsbury ....

From Child Okeford to St. Alban's Head
Or Hope Cove to the mighty Durdle Door
Hardy's county is of a boundless beauty
While abundant wild flowers carpet sweet Dorset's floor ....

Corfe Castle in the twilight, Ballard Head at break of day
A morning strolling happily by the River Stour
Surrounded always by gentle undulating countryside
Where a glorious day becomes one magical hour.

BEWITCHING NAMES

Bulbarrow Hill and southward bound
Where valley springs with 'ere a sound
And westward stroll or skip or stride
On to that place called Piddletrenthide ....
It lies in the valley of the lush Piddle, Puddle or Trent
From its waters and banks village names are thus lent ....
Piddlehinton and Puddletown in a sweet homely huddle
While martyrs' memory remind us of Aff-and-Tolpuddle ....

APPLE BLOSSOM TIME

Churches mellow in purbeck stone nestle in the soft valley
Where birdsong cascades upon the sweet silent air
Mingling with the heady perfume of trees voluptuous with blossom
While we for the present are intoxicated by this beauty
Time pauses for a single moment in its relentless progress
And we stand as still as the stone itself in homage and gratitude ....

ON THIS DAY

On this day some one will be born
Yet some one else will pass away
Some one will smile and be happy
While some one else will be consumed with anger
Some one will laugh in the sunshine
While someone else will cry in the darkness
Some one will wilt in the heat
While some one else will shiver in the cold
Some one will wish for solitude
While some one else will crave company
Some one's heart will be full of love for another
While some one else will be seeking a divorce
Some one will be plotting revenge
While some one else will wonder how they can ever repay a kindness
Some one, this day, will be racked with pain
While some one else knows not the meaning of illness ....
But the wheel of fortune grinds its unceasing circle
Another hand of cards is dealt
Another day will dawn
And suddenly the fugitive becomes the hunter
While today's sorrowing will become tomorrow's fortunate ....
Blessed be the poor in spirit
For they shall inherit the earth.

A THOUSAND VOICES

This England of a thousand voices
Her southern lilts and northern brogues
Of rounded vowels and endless word themes
Changing accents where 'ere ye go.

Old timers from a Dorset village
Will trouble to understand the Lancastrian tongue
While Black Country men will rival the Cockneys
Never the same from one to one.

The charm of a land where birthright dictates
How you will think or sound
The richness of the west or the quality of the east
A wealth of variety is found.

And should you from one wish to go
Or to a foreign county defect
Be sure, my friend, you'll never completely lose
Your birthplace dialect!

POOLE HARBOUR

Pause, stranger, as you stroll Poole harbourside
Please observe the beauty before you
I bid you – halt your stride
And gaze upon a panorama not to be measured in worth
That which glimpses for us a vision
A piece of heaven on earth ....
Pause, stranger, on the brow of Evening Hill
To watch the waters twinkle at Sunset
Drink of that scene of splendour at your will
Brownsea Island lies before you
Seeming not a hop or skip away
While bobbing boats and majestic yachts
An artist's dream portray ....
King Canute sailed into Poole Harbour
The history books tell us in 1015
Did someone stand as we stand now
Gazing upon this wondrous scene
The second largest natural harbour in the world
Our geography books inform
But they don't speak of breathtaking beauty
From sunrise through to dawn ....

PRECIOUS MOMENTS AT SHILLINGSTONE FAIR

My precious moments are corked in bottles
And neatly row the shelves of time
While now and then I savour those moments
Uncorking memory bottles as valuable casks of wine
And as time relentlessly disappears
Those precious moments grow sweeter
With the journey of every passing year.

It's strange how certain scenes we see
We know we shall never forget
While somewhere some thing strikes a chord
And our brain locks in to set
One of these moments is with me now
And as I write again I see
That little lady so old and frail
Sitting in front of me.

It was a blustery day at Shillingstone
The time of their annual Fair
She was with a group of others
All bound in large wheelchairs
Just like a tiny bird she was
So delicate and small
You felt you'd like to hold her close
Let no danger her befall ....

Her hair was as white as virgin snow
Her skin the colour of clotted cream
While she herself was bent and torn
A slender reed bowed o'er a stream
But she wore a dress of pale lavender
And how it pricked my eyes to see
That on her finger was a band of gold
Someone's sweetheart she would always be.

A hurdy-gurdy was playing old-fashioned tunes
And the music rent the air
So happy and jolly the music rang forth
That day at Shillingstone Fair
And as they drew closer the lady must have heard
For suddenly in her chair she leaned up
Ah, the expression on her face was one of sheer joy
Old eyes lit with magic and hope.

She nodded her head and danced her arms
While she laughed and laughed with such glee
That little old lady was young again
Reliving an era we could not see
And from that lady's lovely smile
I knew that the tune was familiar
And transported her back over the years
Where her own precious memories linger.

IN PENSIVE MOOD

In pensive mood I write from the old town of Sherborne
Where I am recalling favourite scenes ....
Reminiscences and colours intertwine
To such a great degree
That an overriding thought comes to play
Which even surprises me ....

The blend of colours that are counties
I may have lost you, so I'll explain
If every county has a colour
Mixed, or patterned, but never plain ....
Sussex is tawny and opal white
Hampshire boasts every shade of green
While Devon is ruddy and Cornwall silver
Do you see now what I mean ....

But Dorset .... ah, Dorset .... which shade?
When sapphire, silver, golden and dazzling white are its cliffs
While its seas are the everchanging blues
Amber to pale sunrise are its castles and churches
Its heathlands stretch purple and wine
Tawny to jade run the hills and downs
River valleys, sheltered hamlets are as an emerald so fine
While brilliant and multi-coloured are the cottage garden homes
Making sweet Dorset as myriad as sun and moonshine ....